To my dear friend,

with wishes of peace

DICTATED BY THE SPIRIT
JOANNA DE ÂNGELIS

PSYCHOGRAPHED BY
DIVALDO PEREIRA FRANCO

HAPPY LIFE

SALVADOR
3rd ed. – 2016

© Copyright 1992 by
"Pathway to Redemption Spiritist Center"
(Centro Espírita Caminho da Redenção)
3rd edition in English - 200 copies
Original title: Vida Feliz (Brazil, 1992)
Translation and revision: Claudia Dealmeida and Darrel Kimble
Desktop publishing: Eduardo Lopez
Cover: Ailton Bosco
Editorial Supervision: Luciano de Castilho Urpia

Cordination and Graphic Production:
LIVRARIA ESPÍRITA ALVORADA EDITORA
Phone: +55 71 3409-8312 / 13 – Salvador – Bahia - Brazil
E-mail: <leal@mansaodocaminho.com.br>
Homepage: www.mansaodocaminho.com.br

International Cataloging in Publication (CIP) Data
Source Cataloging
Biblioteca Joanna de Ângelis

F825	FRANCO, Divaldo. *Happy Life*. 3rd ed. / Dictated by the Spirit Joanna de Ângelis [psichographed by] Divaldo Pereira Franco. Salvador: LEAL, 2016. 224 p. ISBN: 978-1-936547-67-8 1. Spiritism 2. Moral reflections I. Title CDD: 133.93

ALL RIGHTS RESERVED: all rights concerning the reproduction, copying, public communication and economic use of this work are reserved, singly and exclusively, for the Centro Espírita Caminho da Redenção (CECR). Any partial or total reproduction, in any form, and by any means or process, is forbidden, unless express authorization has been granted in advance, in accordance with terms of Law 9.610/98.

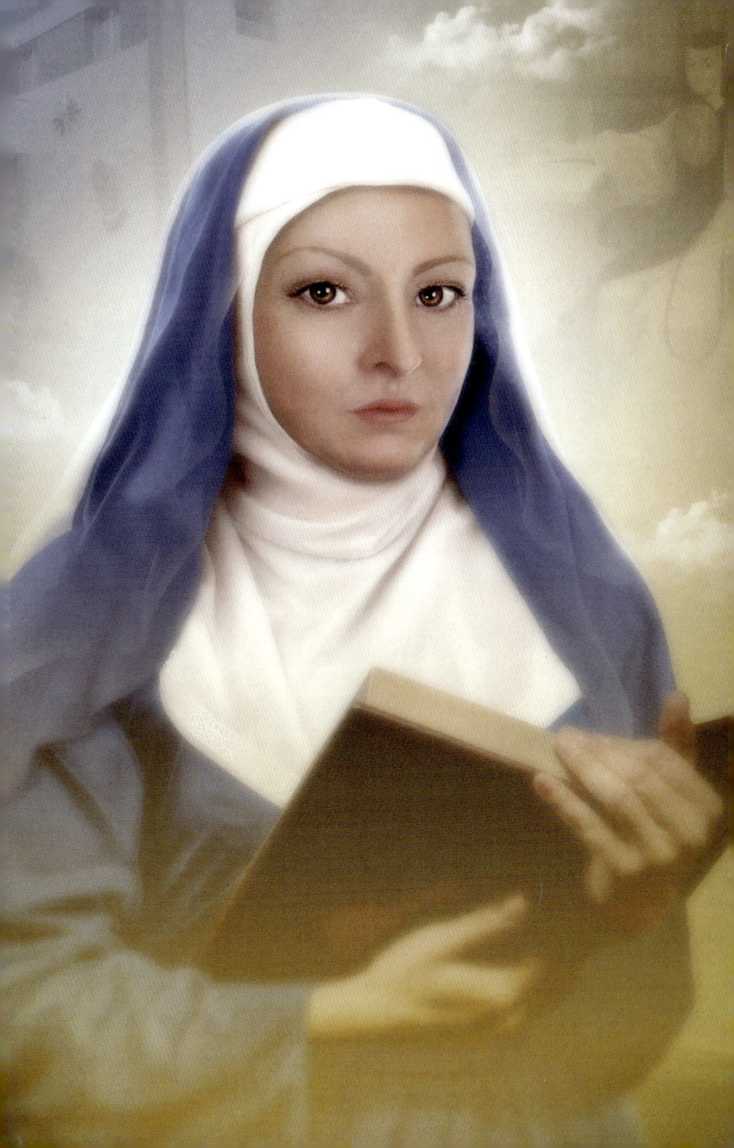

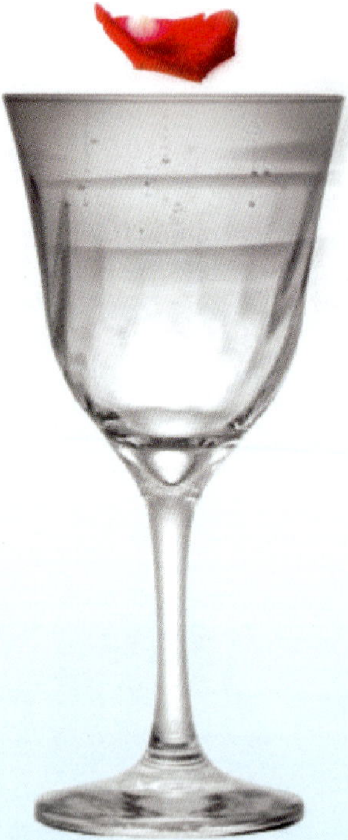

HAPPY LIFE

The ancient Persian city of Ecbatana was home to the **Silent** academy, a gathering place where the sages of the time used silence and meditation to solve problems that were presented to them.

It was during one such gathering that an eminent thinker by the name of Dr. Zeb presented his candidacy to compete for one of the vacancies.

The president received Dr. Zeb in silence, walked up to a nearby board and proceeded to write the number 1000 with a zero to the left, implying Zeb's present worth to the academy.

Unfazed, Dr. Zeb wiped off the zero and switched it to the right of the number, thereby increasing its value tenfold.

Impressed, the president reached for a crystal glass brimming with water, so full that another drop would have certainly caused it to overflow.

Unperturbed, the candidate plucked a petal from a beautiful rose decorating the room and laid it on the water, which remained both undisturbed and more beautiful than before.

Due to his praiseworthy response, Dr. Zeb was accepted as a member of the Academy of sages.

In view of the considerable number of books written about rules of conduct and moral and evangelical guidelines, one more might seem like a zero to the left.

However, on account of the many hearts and minds seeking guidance, help, inspiration and spiritual support, we gathered 200 succinct and familiar topics to present to our readers in a straightforward and practical manner. As always, we request Jesus' kind blessing for this endeavor.

Joanna de Ângelis/Divaldo Franco

It is our hope that this simple little book may become like the rose petal that Dr. Zeb placed on the glass brimming with water, breathing meaning, beauty and life into the physical existence of all who read it.

Joanna de Ângelis
Salvador, February 20, 1988

I

Greet your day with a prayer of gratitude. You are alive.

While there is life, opportunities for growth and happiness abound.

Each day is a new blessing from God, proof of His love for you.

As you pass the hours, cultivate optimism and well-being.

II

Regard work as the best way to progress.

Those who do not work surrender to moral and spiritual paralysis.

Those who do not invest in work's liberating action are a dead weight on society's economy.

Work is life.

III

As much as possible, immerse your mind in study.

Study rids the mind of ignorance and provides discernment.

Study and work are the wings that foster evolution.

Knowledge is the message of life.

Studying is not limited to just the classroom, however.

Life itself is an open book that teaches all who are willing to learn.

IV

Patience is a virtue that will help you acquire physical, spiritual and social assets.

It teaches us how to wait when we cannot have what we want right away.

Never become impatient.

Patience will help you overcome everything.

Joanna de Ângelis/Divaldo Franco

Grant others the same rights and favors that you expect from them.

Selfishness is a disease that poisons the soul.

The person next to you yearns for freedom just as you do.

Remember to never thwart someone else's opportunity.

Learn to share of what you have received.

VI

When in doubt, choose the approach that is the least damaging to yourself and your neighbor.

Avoid running the risk of seriously harming others.

Act calmly and be assured that your action will have an impact on others according to its emotion and content.

Joanna de Ângelis/Divaldo Franco

VII

Do not be overly ambitious.

Be mindful of the saying, "Do not let your reach exceed your grasp."

Unchecked ambition leads to unhappiness and ultimately to madness.

See to it that you work for what is actually necessary and share the surplus with those who need it.

VIII

Always live in peace.

A clear conscience, one that is unencumbered with remorse about the past and unafraid in relation to the future breeds harmony.

No external circumstances can disturb a serene heart that beats to the rhythm of duty rightly fulfilled.

Finding peace deserves every bit of effort on your part.

Joanna de Ângelis/Divaldo Franco

IX

Maintain your emotional composure in all situations.

An unstable nervous system means a life in disarray.

Should difficulties threaten to throw you off balance, turn to prayer.

Prayer is the effective medicine for all the ailments of the soul.

X

Organize your schedule so that you can spend your time appropriately.

Every task must be seen to at the right time.

Disorganization in carrying it out not only harms its order but compromises its quality.

Perform your duties calmly and uninterruptedly one after the other.

XI

Be a friend to all.

Friendship is a treasure of the Spirit and is meant to be shared.

Like the sun, it shines and bestows joy upon all who receive it.

There is a critical shortage of friends on the earth, which breeds conflict, mistrust, instability and insecurity.

When people lack friendship in their lives, they put themselves in danger.

Be a kind friend even if you are experiencing misunderstanding and hardship.

XII

Never repay a wrong with revenge.

Bad people are sick but do not know it.

Give them medicine that will lessen their confusion and resist the "eye for an eye" approach.

If others offend you, that is their problem.

But if you offend others, the situation reverses and the problem becomes yours.

The offender is always worse off.

Be mindful of this and go your way in peace.

XIII

Always put your trust in Divine Help.

Should you feel besieged with no way out, help will arrive from God.

Never doubt the Divine Paternity.

God watches over and helps you, not always as you would like, but in the way that is best for your true happiness.

At times, it may seem that Divine Help will not arrive or will arrive too late.

But afterward – if you waited – you will see that it did arrive a short time before.

XIV

Use every opportunity to act with utmost dignity.

Some people wait for extraordinary moments and special occasions that most likely will not materialize.

It is not so much what you do but how you do it that will make you invaluable.

A giant tree begins as a tiny seed.

The cosmos is the result of invisible particles and molecules.

Be great in small matters so that you are not small in great ones.

Joanna de Ângelis/Divaldo Franco

XV

"Only wolves fall into wolf traps," teaches the Gospel of Jesus.

So, do not assent to the thorn of humiliation or dishonor when you are hurt or slandered.

You are what you cultivate inside, and not what you are blamed for.

You will not be any better just because you are praised, nor will you be any worse just because you are criticized.

Stay true to yourself, honorable and discreet, in your quest for inner growth.

XVI

In your vocabulary, replace bad words with good ones.

Vulgar words may be fashionable but they *poison the heart*.

Words are life's instruments for communication and understanding, not weapons of aggression, violence and vulgarity.

The poor use of words corrupts the mind and degrades the person.

Words manifest an individual's moral quality.

Because there are bad people who are well-spoken, it is not right for you, being good, to express yourself with bad words.

Joanna de Ângelis/Divaldo Franco

XVII

Keep your thoughts in a wholesome and optimistic rhythm.

The mind is a powerful dynamo.

According to how you think, you will attract similar vibratory responses.

Those who cultivate sickness always become sick.

Those who persevere in health always overcome infirmities.

Think rightly and God will inspire you to find the best solutions.

An uplifting, good thought is an unspoken prayer that never goes unheard.

XVIII

Constant rebelliousness throws the mind, body and soul out of balance.

It is not the flesh that is weak – it is the Spirit that is rebellious.

Keep your energy in check. Don't let it throw you off-balance.

Rebelliousness emits a poison that unsettles everyone nearby.

A rebellious person inspires neither friendship nor compassion.

Keep calm no matter what happens.

What is not yet resolved will soon be.

Joanna de Ângelis/Divaldo Franco

XIX

Be tolerant of others' flaws and do not expose them to the festival of gossip.

We all make mistakes.

Wise are those who, when they err, learn to act correctly.

Should someone fall, offer your hand instead of criticism.

Nobody fails intentionally, and when they do, ignorance, their cruel enemy, gains the upper hand.

Even then, the one who has failed needs assistance, not reproach.

XX

Never be complacent about what you have done badly.

Acknowledge your right to make mistakes, but rectify them immediately.

Bitterness, rage and violence must give way to joy, benevolence and peace.

You have reincarnated to grow and be happy.

Walk away from emotional dysfunction and ascend the steps that will lead you to victory over yourself.

Those who are unable to tame their negative inclinations become victims of the resultant disorderliness.

Joanna de Ângelis/Divaldo Franco

XXI

Love is the tonic of life.

When centered on sex and the lower passions, it becomes a prison and no longer the uplifting, dignifying and liberating sentiment that it really is.

Examine your sentiments regarding love to see if they bring you peace or disharmony. By their nature, you will know if you actually love or merely desire.

True love overcomes selfishness and always works on behalf of the loved one.

Therefore, love without enslaving those to whom you are devoted, or becoming enslaved to them.

XXII

Jealousy in your behavior is a sign of imbalance.

Jealousy can never be the salt that seasons love.

Insecurity and mistrust are the manifestation of jealousy.

When it takes root in a relationship, it causes nightmares and harmful perturbations.

Overcome your jealousy, loving with tranquility and trusting in peace.

If your loved one doesn't live up to your expectations, move on. It is his or her loss.

XXIII

Avoid altercations, for they are useless.

Between contenders, the person who refuses to get involved in fruitless arguments is always right.

The only product of verbal clashes and violent altercations is hostility, which is difficult to amend.

Words spoken in anger rarely express what a person is actually thinking.

They demonstrate the person's state of disharmony and the urge to crush his or her opponent.

Express your ideas calmly. If the other person disagrees, remain silent and give him or her over to time, which teaches us all unhurriedly.

XXIV

The body and the mind need rest.

However, be careful that it does not turn into idleness or laziness.

After work, it is right to recharge your energy by switching activities, resting or sleeping.

Too much rest, however, corrupts a person's character and weakens the muscle fibers, designed for movement and action.

So, allow for enough rest but do not overdo it.

XXV

When asked about another person, always give positive feedback.

If this is not possible because the person acts reprehensibly, keep silent or speak benevolently. Avoid aggravating his or her situation or making it more well-known.

You are not an overseer of other people's behavior. You cannot know if yesterday's offender might now be in recovery.

Let your opinions always be uplifting and your words helpful.

XXVI

Calm your longing for constant change.

God has put you in the best place for your spiritual and moral progress.

Your home life, your current job and the city where you live are opportunities for your evolution.

"A rolling stone gathers no moss," is a popular saying.

People who are constantly on the move do not mature or accomplish anything.

Fulfill your tasks in a timely manner wherever you may be. After careful meditation, choose the path that is best for you.

XXVII

Don't ignore the value and power of prayer.

Just as the body needs adequate nutrition to survive, so does the Spirit as matter's life-giving agent.

Prayer is high-octane *fuel* for the harmony of the Spirit.

Make prayer a habit. Incorporate it into your daily routine and you will see its benefits.

Don't deny yourself the bread of life, which is sincere, heartfelt prayer.

XXVIII

Be kind to children.

They need opportunity and love to succeed.

These citizens in the making do not know the struggles that lie ahead.

Offer them kindness and transmit to them your trust in the humankind that you represent.

Don't frighten or mistreat them.

Anyone who saw that little boy in Nazareth long ago, playing without a care amongst other children, never could have imagined that He was the Architect of the Earth, our Model and Guide.

XXIX

Show kindness and gratitude to all, especially the elderly.

Old age is an inevitable stage that you too will reach, should death not claim your body sooner.

During this difficult phase, strength diminishes, organs weaken, memory fades, and physical and emotional dependency sets in.

The presence of the elderly may be wearisome; however, they have a wealth of experience to offer in return for the resources you can provide.

XXX

Every vice enslaves and kills.

Don't indulge in *social drinking*, a veritable gateway to alcoholism. Don't become a smoker, for while it may seem stylish and elegant, it will bind you in the shackles of deadly tobacco dependency.

Gambling, sex, gluttony and off-color joking – to name just a few – start small but end up as moral prisons, if not actual jail time.

A healthy lifestyle makes for a joyful, long life for those who pursue it.

XXXI

Be a peacemaker.

Live in peace and promote it wherever you may be.

Widespread turmoil and fighting could be prevented or at least circumvented if people would practice mutual goodwill.

Receiving an offense in silence, meeting an attack with forgiveness, or diverting a blow would prevent many conflicts that erupt in flames of hatred.

Believe in the power of nonviolence and peace will blossom in your heart and the hearts of those around you.

XXXII

Spread the hope of better days to come.

Never before has the need for the olive branch of hope been as great as it is today.

Hope fuels ideals and gives people the courage to tackle their own self-renewal, even when everything seems lost.

Hope upholds the hero and the saint in their lofty purposes.

Enshrining it within you, you will never get discouraged, nor will you feel forsaken when the circumstances call for testimony and solitude.

Joanna de Ângelis/Divaldo Franco

XXXIII

Pity the ungrateful. They have suffocated their most beautiful sentiments in the vapors of pride.

Gratitude is a dignified emotion that should reign within all who reap life's benefits.

We are all indebted to someone or to many people who have helped us in tough times.

Help received at just the right time is responsible for all the good that has come your way, and should impel you to a state of perennial gratitude.

Be grateful in every situation.

XXXIV

Keep cheerfulness as part of your conduct.

A grouchy demeanor implies distress, discontent and annoyance.

You can act rightly and be effective without wearing a mask of sullenness.

Cheerfully and joyfully spread good humor all around you, radiating the well-being that fills your heart.

The treasure of cheerful behavior is worth the happiness it bestows on others.

Joanna de Ângelis/Divaldo Franco

XXXV

Allocate some of your time to serving your community out of fraternal charity.

Free time is a dangerous mental space. Offer such time to your neighbor or to some charitable organization dedicated to rebuilding lives.

Small contributions produce the miracle of grand achievements.

Never excuse yourself from doing volunteer work.

There is much suffering waiting for help and understanding.

XXXVI

Make a vow to yourself to fulfill every commitment in an orderly, unhurried manner.

People who value what they do lend it beauty and meaning, and thus do it better.

Every job is useful, no matter how menial it may seem.

Both the universe and the worm, so different and contrasting, are important within the Divine Creation.

Perform each task gladly and respectfully.

XXXVII

Never deceive anyone.

Life is the great debt collector and it will demand payment in full.

What you do to others will always return to you.

The harvest always follows the planting.

You will reap what you have sown.

People that mislead, lie, or betray harm primarily themselves, first by disrespecting themselves, and second by deserving the consequences of their reproachable conduct.

Be honest with yourself and, consequently, with your neighbor.

XXXVIII

Use the truth for the purpose of helping and never as a weapon of aggression or retaliation.

Truth is like a diamond: it requires appropriate storage for safekeeping, and when thrown at someone, it does not wound him or her.

Your truth might not be the actual truth, or at least the whole truth.

Save it for the right time, when it might be useful to restore someone's dignity or bring him or her back from the edge of madness and illusion.

Joanna de Ângelis/Divaldo Franco

XXXIX

Don't neglect people who are in more difficult and humble situations than your own.
Befriend them.
It is easy to share in other people's joys, successes and enviable situations.
The ideal is to be everyone's friend.
Wealth, power, health and youth are all fleeting.
Make love your most valuable asset and offer it to all.

XL

When someone is being accused, keep quiet.

When events are made public, there are always antecedents unknown to the majority.

Things are not always as they *seem*, but they are in keeping with their inner values.

Don't echo the accusations.

Offenders and transgressors at least deserve compassion and a chance to right their wrongs.

XLI

Start making amends the moment you realize you are in the wrong.

Forget about surrendering to discouragement or remorse.

Just as you must not persist in the wrongdoing, you must not beat yourself up in regret.

Remorse's only role is making one aware of the wrong.

Forgive yourself. Take heart and begin the task of personal rebalance by lessening and repairing the harm you have caused.

XLII

In today's chaotic world, take some time for silence. It will translate into inner quietude.

Agitation, commotion and non-stop chatter disharmonize the emotional centers of balance.

Listen more than you speak.

Think before expressing your opinion.

Walk away from commotion, preserving your peace of mind.

This is the right approach for every moment of your life.

Joanna de Ângelis/Divaldo Franco

XLIII

Happiness is possible for you.

Believe it is and strive to achieve it.

Don't put your happiness in people, places or things so as not to be disappointed.

Happiness is an inner state resulting from the well-being that leading a dignified and serene life provides.

Even in the absence of money, social standing and health, happiness is possible if you practice resignation and put your trust in God.

XLIV

Love yourself more.

Of course, this does not mean being selfish, greedy or noxious.

Self-love implies self-respect, striving for the higher achievements of life, the lofty yearnings of the heart.

Try to set up a simple self-love plan and follow it.

Stay enthusiastic and be certain that you are destined for the Great Light. Let your most high-minded aspirations shine.

In all things, always choose the "best part," moving beyond what is detrimental, harmful and degrading.

XLV

The body requires care to stay healthy.

Neglect, under any pretense, constitutes an act of rebellion against God, who has given the body as a vehicle for inner growth and moral elevation.

Abstain from paying way too much attention to it, as is the case with many people, but preserve, protect and love it to extend its useful existence.

St. Francis of Assisi referred to the body as *Brother Donkey*, for it carries our soul while on the earth. As such, it deserves tender love and care.

XLVI

Eat to live. Avoid emotional eating, which makes people live to eat.

Many more people die from overeating or eating irregularly than from starvation.

The extravagant, wastefulness of a few is responsible for the hunger of many.

Food is a blessing for bodily existence. However, complicated concoctions and extravagant dishes are an unjustifiable passion, a harmful vice.

Use food wisely and frugally so you may live a long life in optimal health.

Joanna de Ângelis/Divaldo Franco

XLVII

Follow the course of events without apprehension.

Neither your anxiety nor fear will alter the course of time.

Wait for what is to come without the suffering of anticipation.

What you expect to happen might actually happen, though not exactly in the way you had envisioned, for life follows a plan of incessant changes and transformations.

So wait with inner harmony, without agitation and dread.

XLVIII

Listen carefully and attentively.

Don't rush to interrupt as if you already understood.

Some people struggle to express themselves, so they are hard to comprehend.

After listening, discuss the matter to make sure you have grasped it, if circumstances allow.

Good listeners have better comprehension.

Listening is an art that is seldom practiced.

Joanna de Ângelis/Divaldo Franco

XLIX

Many people relish spreading bad news, conveying unsound ideas and opinions. They are couriers of unrest.

Be very discreet when with them. They will test your resolve with gossip, only to distort your comments and pass them on to someone else.

In such circumstances, silence is the cotton that dampens the noise of the spread of growing evil.

Those that bring you the garbage of slander are not your friends.

God has endowed you with willpower.

If yours is weak, it is because of lack of exercise.

All moral and organic functions require practice to readily obey mental commands.

Start training by correcting minor bad habits, gradually moving on to greater challenges.

By disciplining your will, you will achieve your present existence's greatest goals.

Should you fail at first, do not give up.

LI

People who hold grudges gather moral filth and subsequently end up getting sick.

You should not suffer because of wrongs done to you.

If someone wants you to be unhappy, live joyfully instead.

If someone wants to throw you off balance, remain stable.

If an adversary plots to bring you down, keep your inner peace.

The greatest pain for those who seek to make others unhappy is to see them unfazed by it.

Be smart. Don't wear yourself out pointlessly.

LII

True forgiveness always includes erasing the offense from one's memory.

If you forgive but keep referring to the incident, you are actually keeping it alive.

Work on the personal weakness that keeps you fixated on the painful event and be grateful for the opportunity to forgive.

How would we evolve without moral trials?

Today's forgiveness will be your sponsor tomorrow when you yourself need mercy and forgiveness from someone else.

Forgiveness is always best for the forgiver.

Do so always and you will live.

LIII

Bad thoughts poison the soul.

They attract pessimism along with bad and disturbed Spirits.

Lock your mind on positive, enlightening ideas and higher goals, from which well-being and the zest for life derive.

What you persistently think about will materialize sooner or later.

Events are first shaped in the mind and later manifested in the physical body.

Focus on the good and bathe in the light of love.

LIV

Be kind and good without becoming subservient.

Humility is a lofty virtue that does not coexist with vile situations.

Incorruptible, humility enriches people with spiritual values that make them strong in their apparent weakness and powerful in their poverty.

Socrates, Christ and Gandhi are humility's greatest examples and evolution's most beautiful exponents.

Stricken down by crazed murderers, they preferred to die rather than to yield, remaining immortal in their grand victory.

LV

Don't trade tomorrow's peaceful conscience for today's corrupting thrills.

If something is immoral, it will never bring you peace. Fleeting and rapacious, it burns the body with the acid of discontentment and the embittered conscience with the darkness of remorse.

It is better to be wanting than regretful.

What you have not yet endured does not torment you, and what you lack now will come later without drawbacks.

LVI

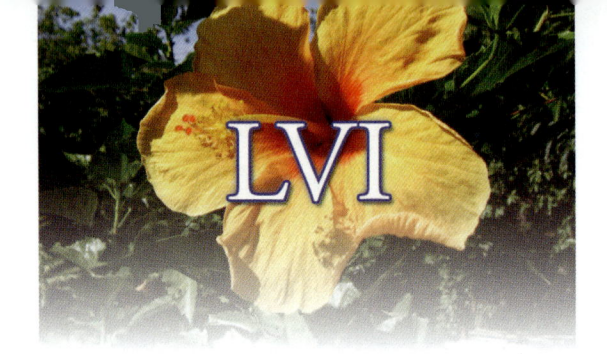

Ill-gotten wins are a fallacy.

They leave a bitter taste.

Being unjust, they wound others and in actuality they benefit nobody.

Those who construct on their neighbor's land end up losing the building.

Happiness at the expense of someone else's tears will never be true happiness.

Choose your goals mindfully and pursue them only when proven legally and morally sound.

Joanna de Ângelis/Divaldo Franco

LVII

Channel your energy properly so that it does not turn into arrogance and aggression.

You can and should be assertive, just never aggressive.

It is reasonable to feel happy about your resources, just not boastful.

Should the desire for retaliation cloud your judgment, act firmly but judiciously.

The power that builds also destroys.

The hard-nosed and the high-strung end up alone, with frazzled nerves.

LVIII

Be compassionate toward the weak.

Lend them a helping hand in every situation.

In addition to their physical frailties, they are shy and dependent, for they are fully aware of being energy depleted.

Help them with a kindly smile of friendship and your promise of silent support. Treat them in a way that makes them feel secure.

Put yourself in their shoes and offer them what you would like to receive if you were in their situation.

LIX

Keep up your courage as you struggle, no matter what the situation is.

Some pathways are less difficult to travel, yet all pose a challenge.

There is an assumption that if you work for the good of others, you yourself are exempt from obstacles and difficulties.

That is a fallacy. People are the same everywhere.

St. Vincent de Paul, who did so much for the poor, declared that they were "very demanding and ungrateful."

So, have courage always.

LX

Meditate on death from time to time.

Death claims enemies and loved ones, and could claim you, yourself, at any given moment.

Prepare yourself every day as if it were your last day on earth.

By getting used to the idea of death, it will not hurt you when it comes for you or a loved one.

St. Francis of Assisi waited for death with the same serenity with which he *weeded his garden*.

LXI

Your ownership in relation to your earthly assets is relative.

In a transitory world, what is yours now will have changed hands tomorrow.

Use but do not abuse the resources at your disposal.

Do not become a slave to what you hold for a few moments and you will not suffer when it passes to someone else.

The only permanent assets are the treasures of the sentiments, culture and virtue.

The Gospel teaches "Store up treasures in heaven."

LXII

Your experience is an asset acquired over time as you move through life's lessons in your process of evolution.

A road traveled is a road known.

In light of such an achievement, you discover that there is a huge gap between theory and practice.

Think more before you act, making calm, level-headed decisions.

When you act on impulse, you are subject to making big mistakes.

Certain events happen at their appropriate time; even so, a wise person sets the time for lofty achievements.

Joanna de Ângelis/Divaldo Franco

LXIII

The most important things in life are valued only after they are gone.

More often than not, people do things automatically without appreciating the invaluable Divine Resources.

Health, sleep, reason, digestion, breathing, sensory organs and mobility are all God-given treasures; however, you do not realize their magnificence and you waste them greedily to acquire lesser assets.

Stop and think about the meaning of each one of these gifts and guard them against things that consume them.

LXIV

Go for a walk outdoors.

Calmly, rediscover nature, which has blessed your life.

Unwind and exit the surrounding turmoil by letting your imagination soar.

Avoid crowded places and breathe the fresh air of the woods, the mountains, the sea…

Revisit concepts; relax and bless life in whatever form it takes for you.

Your present existence is plentiful with what you need to be happy.

Joanna de Ângelis/Divaldo Franco

LXV

"Seek the middle ground," the saying goes.

This is an appeal for moderation, without extremes.

Whenever you get impassioned and assume an extreme posture, you make the same mistakes that you criticize in others.

In any discussion, taking the middle ground is best, not out of convenience or fear, but because you don't have all the facts.

Balanced conduct is revealed at the time decisions are made.

LXVI

Be open to new concepts and ideas.

Talk them over and compare them to what you already know and think, making the best of the new information.

Sound ideas reinvigorate your emotions, supplying the sentiments with motivation and enthusiasm.

No one is so wise or complete that he or she can dispense with further learning or additional contributions for inner growth.

Learn more by being receptive to fresh input.

Joanna de Ângelis/Divaldo Franco

LXVII

Things that overexcite one's mind, body and emotions should be avoided.

While the soft melodies of good music are soothing, there are others that are meant to rouse lust and violence; they have a disturbing effect on one's nerves.

Good books instruct and educate, while books with outrageous and sensual content corrupt and alter one's moral values for the worse.

Principled conversations uplift, whereas vulgar ones debase one's character.

Steer clear of the wave of indignity that has taken a hold of people and the world.

LXVIII

When you are ignorant about a subject, just say so.

You are not expected to know everything.

Honesty regarding one's limitations is much appreciated. Even when you are already informed about what someone is trying to tell you, listen patiently. It will give you the chance to compare it with what you already know, enhancing or rectifying it.

People who come across as very well-informed oftentimes have knowledge that is only skin-deep.

Listening is always profitable.

Joanna de Ângelis/Divaldo Franco

LXIX

Parenthood is a major responsibility.

Humans are born with the destiny they themselves have forged in past reincarnations.

Even so, they will always be affected by their parents' examples.

Thus, the first school is the home, and the home is the result of the behavior of the parents, who should put forth the effort to make it pleasant, honorable and rich in peace.

Bless your children with your words and deeds; be their friend in every situation.

Children – like the rest of us – are from God and you will have to answer for this loan, given to you to educate.

LXX

When it comes to moral values, no one can reap someone else's crop.

We are all our own heirs.

Immortal Spirits that we are, we evolve step by step as students in a school of love, repeating the lesson when wrong or being promoted when right.

Thus, one physical existence follows another, picking up where we left off, correcting what we have done wrongly or starting a completely new experience.

What love doesn't accomplish, however, suffering certainly will.

LXXI

You are immersed in the ocean of God's love.

You are never alone.

God is within and all around you.

Discover Him and let Him lead you with wisdom.

You are His heir, owner of the universe.

Let His love permeate you completely, guiding your will and your steps, enabling you to grow with little or no suffering.

In God you find everything, attaining completeness.

LXXII

Rejoice at every opportunity to evolve.

Suffering met with resignation loses intensity; endured in silence, it passes more quickly.

You will never suffer what you do not deserve, just as you cannot live on the earth as an exception, without facing suffering.

God's laws are the same for everyone.

Replacing love in short supply, suffering is the teacher that propels us forward.

Joanna de Ângelis/Divaldo Franco

LXXIII

The wounds of the soul are the most mortifying.

External injuries heal easily; inner ones take much longer.

Bathe in the waters of faith in God, of patience, humility, forgiveness and love. Prevent hatred, selfishness, rebellion, or sorrow from bruising your soul.

Many physical ailments originate in the Spirit wounded by emotional unrest or the caustic effect of moral flaws.

Safeguard your inner workings from the relentless assaults of vice and irresponsibility.

LXXIV

Don't fret over what you cannot finish right away.

Do what is possible in terms of effort and dedication and avoid the discouragement that comes with apparent failure.

When a task exceeds your capacity or when circumstances get in the way, your real task is to remain calm.

Those who do all they can, achieve the most.

… And what you cannot finish now, you will finish tomorrow if you remain faithful to your commitment.

Joanna de Ângelis/Divaldo Franco

LXXV

Avoid being overly sensitive.

No matter what path you take, you will always find friendly and unfriendly individuals.

It is not worth taking offense and brooding in dissatisfaction.

All progress is subject to hurdles and difficulties; they are challenges and reasons for pressing on.

A journey without problems becomes monotonous and boring.

You grow due to the struggles you face.

Stay cheerful even when faced with icy or exasperating people.

LXXVI

Stop complaining all the time so that you will not become a *persona non grata*.

Keeping company with complainers is very unpleasant. They find fault with everything, and they want the world to revolve around them in conformance with their way of seeing things.

Since you cannot change others, you must work tirelessly on your own self-improvement.

If everything displeases you and you find yourself complaining all the time, watch out. It is an attitude of someone who is out of sorts with life and him or herself.

You must tolerate yourself and learn to be tolerant of others.

LXXVII

If only for today, at least, place beauty before your eyes to brighten your outlook on life.

Shake off last night's troubles and set out to face people and the world with some measure of goodwill.

You will feel inwardly renewed and your surroundings will seem much more pleasant.

Goodwill extended to others will return to you as warmth and fellowship.

Face the new day committed to winning and claiming your good place in the world.

LXXVIII

When an obstacle appears blocking your way, waste no time. Stop and go around it.

If some unforeseen problem threatens your tranquility, don't feel distressed.

Silence your rebelliousness and work on solving it as best you can.

If someone you love is acting strangely toward you or has forsaken you, keep calm. The rebel and the deserter have already lost their reason due to their impulsivity.

Remain at peace.

What you lose now, you will gain later.

If you behave with dignity, whatever happens to you will be for your own benefit in the future.

Joanna de Ângelis/Divaldo Franco

LXXIX

Make your hours a rosary of blessings.

By wisely investing your time in uplifting endeavors, you will amass unimaginable happiness.

If you waste your time, you will never get it back.

Time that passes never returns. It is like water under the bridge.

Eternity is composed of seconds, and time, measured in hours, is a gift from God to provide you with well-being.

Work without discouragement and accumulate your hours of useful service.

LXXX

You could do more for humanity if you wanted to.

Reach out to the fallen. Say a kind word to someone. Offer a fraternal smile to the lonely. Give a flower to a friend. Make a sad person smile. Envelop the downtrodden in tenderness…

Coins of love are worth more than bank notes if offered from the heart and at the right time.

No one turns away a friend or scorns a kind gesture.

Strive for the honor of being one of the builders of a better world and a happier society.

LXXXI

Jesus said, "Let not your hearts be troubled," teaching that serenity and trust in God must be the motto of all who desire happiness.

There is never a shortage of reasons for worry, which unsettles one's heart and life.

Human existence is a chance to appreciate eternal values and inner enlightenment.

If you trust God with your life and all your worries, everything will unfold naturally. Should a problem arise, serenity will take control and settle the matter properly.

Therefore, do not let your heart or mind be troubled by misfortune.

LXXXII

When you undertake a commitment, honor it with your presence.

Before you assume any responsibility, think it through to avoid unpleasant situations.

Should something keep you from showing up or attending to it, communicate it ahead of time to avoid inconveniencing those waiting for or counting on you.

Whatever the magnitude of your responsibilities, always fulfill them all.

Joanna de Ângelis/Divaldo Franco

LXXXIII

Don't fear your accusers when they slander you and want to drag you into inglorious battles.

But if you are accused and the fact is true, thank God for the chance to make a timely rectification for your own well-being.

It is always best to right your wrongs while the victim is still around.

Postponed debts grow with accruing interest, thus becoming harder to repay.

LXXXIV

Choose your friends wisely.

Bad company is a liability because it hinders your progress.

No one is so autonomous and complete so as to avoid contamination by those who delight in wrongdoing and vice.

Be kind to bad and irresponsible people, but do not partake of their behavior, activities and their take on life.

Moral infirmities also infect the unwary who come too close.

Joanna de Ângelis / Divaldo Franco

LXXXV

Keep your activities well organized.

Be neither overwhelmed nor negligent in relation to your obligations.

As time allows, fulfill each one to the end.

A disciplined person is a treasure.

People who accomplish tedious and repetitive tasks are fit to undertake greater assignments with assured success.

Being orderly and aware of the fact that life is an endless activity means a step forward on the road of evolution.

LXXXVI

Take a firm stand when it comes to preserving your health.

Many illnesses can be traced back to mental instability, emotional imbalance and negative Spirit-related influences...

Anxiety, fear, pessimism, anger, jealousy and hatred are responsible for yet uncatalogued diseases that ravage people's physical, emotional and mental health.

Strive to maintain your peace-of-mind, cultivating good thoughts that will bring you inestimable benefits.

The quality of your physical existence depends on what you prefer to think about.

Joanna de Angelis/Divaldo Franco

LXXXVII

Advice is only as valuable as your willingness to follow it.

Whenever you struggle with any given subject, seek guidance from a more experienced, better-equipped person. However, leave your own opinion at the door, and do not try to prove it right.

Listen carefully and ponder. Then make what seems to be the best decision.

Moreover, don't let good advice fall on deaf ears.

"Examine everything; hold fast to that which is good," states the Apostle, in the name of the Good.

LXXXVIII

No one will help solve your problems if you do not make an effort to face and solve them yourself.

Someone may lend you money to pay down a debt; nonetheless, the debt persists; only the creditor has changed.

A friend may become your "Simon of Cyrene" but your cross is personal and each person must carry it to his or her liberating Calvary.

Therefore, do not tax your loved ones with your grievances, complaints and struggles.

Try to solve one problem at a time until you have overcome all of them.

Joanna de Ângelis / Divaldo Franco

LXXXIX

If you have nothing helpful to say, say nothing critical.

There are two kinds of conduct: the one that accomplishes and the other that finds fault, criticizing and making other people's lives miserable.

Do what is possible, expecting neither applause nor criticism.

Join the group that operates and speaks with the lofty objective of being useful.

If those who claim to know how things are done would stop talking and start doing, the world would be a different place.

XC

Don't isolate yourself in your social circle.
Loneliness gives bad counsel.
People who isolate themselves from family, work and their community become disturbed.
Fleeing the world hinders the use of reason, leading to a distorted view in relation to people and events.
Humans are social beings, meant to help and learn from one another.
It is in the day-to-day struggles and the course of human activities that the values that must be developed and improved are assessed.

Joanna de Ângelis/Divaldo Franco

XCI

Think in terms of eternal life.

Death is but a change of address.

When the physical tissues become worn out or rend violently, they release the eternal spirit, who returns to the Spirit Homeland.

Everything undergoes transformation.

The body changes and decays, giving life to other material expressions in turn.

However, the spirit being, who temporarily inhabits the body, abandons it to reclaim its intrinsic reality.

Therefore, as you live, know that death can reach you at any moment and that you must prepare yourself for the inevitable journey.

Happy Life

XCII

Don't pin your hopes on entertainment, trips, parties and distractions.

If the opportunity arises to enjoy them, seize it and you will see that such pleasures are fleeting like all others, leaving you hungry for more, in a self-perpetuating cycle.

Some people will go as far as to mortgage their future, resorting to exorbitant loans in order to experience such illusions, which come back as nightmares when it is time to repay the debt.

Seek simple, lasting pleasures: the kind that do not disturb you in the present or enslave you in the future.

XCIII

Make sure that pessimism and rebelliousness do not find shelter in your heart, numbing or frazzling your nerves.

Reconsider unpleasant attitudes and events, taking heart and continuing on your journey in peace.

Your spiritual state has everything to do with the outcome of your aspirations and actions.

When you begin a task with antagonistic feelings or resistance, you have already lost.

Bring the warmth of hope and optimism to all you do and success will be inevitable.

XCIV

Jesus said, "Man does not live by bread alone, but also by God's word."

Concerns relative to food, clothing, housing and social interaction should not come at the expense of one's interest in the spiritual life.

Set time aside daily to nourish yourself with *God's word*.

Bread feeds the body while faith upholds the soul.

Bread strengthens matter, whereas faith dignifies life.

Bread briefly satiates hunger, but faith fulfills our needs for good.

Care for your body and nurture your soul so you may feel complete.

XCV

Rein in the impulses that result from ungoverned instincts; act under the command of reason.

It is true that good sentiments must melt the ice of rational logic, but oftentimes indifference or aggression need the vigilance of reason.

Brain and heart must work together, providing the advantages of both balance and moderation for a healthy life.

Listen with your heart and act with your reason, each in appropriate measure.

XCVI

Whenever possible, be mindful of your personal appearance; neither overdress like a model, nor underdress like a slob.

Clothes are made for the person and not the other way around.

Fashion is a money-making market invention that exploits people's foolishness and immaturity.

A clean outfit that protects the body, even if outdated, is worth more than the latest, oftentimes ridiculous creation.

Do not feel bad for not being in vogue, which is always short-lived.

XCVII

Your suffering is yours alone.

No one will endure it for you.

Friends will sympathize and will look for ways to help you, but the thorn will be imbedded in the flesh of your own soul.

Likewise, your happiness is yours alone.

There will be much laughter and celebration amongst your loved ones, but the elation you feel cannot be shared with anyone else.

That said, as you suffer do not impose your anguish on those around you, just as in joy you cannot make them feel blissful.

XCVIII

Exile evil from the provinces of your life.

Counter sickly thoughts with healthy ones. Rend the vicious web of unjustifiable suspicion with the scissors of trust in others.

It is horrific living life armed against others, seeing primarily their negative side, and detecting their imperfections.

No one on earth is flawless, just as there is no one who does not have some virtue, no matter how bad he or she is.

Look for the good aspect in everyone and you will find yourself well, renewed and agreeable.

Joanna de Ângelis/Divaldo Franco

XCIX

In the end, violent people either annihilate one another or self-destruct.

Peace can solve any antagonistic situation when the contenders are guided by love.

To get rid of an effect we must eliminate its cause.

When violence is the cause, only its antidote – prudence – can counter it.

A peaceful person appeases another; then both alter the behavior of the group, which, in turn, can change the community, and so on.

Do your part to transcend violence.

Don't yell.

No situation calls for yelling, because it makes the situation even worse.

When you speak in a normal tone, the rowdy will become silent so they can hear you.

Should you try to compete with them by yelling too, you will lose your voice and will not be heard.

The voice reveals a person's behavior and emotional state.

We are not referring to the vocal dynamics of professional speaking, which does have its purpose, but to a natural, audible and friendly tone.

Have you heard yourself on tape, especially when upset?

Try it.

CI

You need serenity at every step of the way. Serenity to discern, act and live.

Life rushes at you and changes situations by the minute, requiring constant serenity to avoid trampling on other people.

Those who torment themselves by trying to keep up with the breakneck speed of the times will be crushed because they do not adjust to a situation before jumping to the next.

News and events come and go, causing enormous emotional, mental and physical fatigue.

Seek shelter in serenity, preserving the equipment of your existence, equipment that is meant to be used properly, not abused.

Constant exhaustion, dissatisfaction and bad moods are a big, red flag of danger in your life.

They result from the improper use of your energy and resources, and not taking the time to recover.

Sleep by itself cannot provide enough rest to your body if you are agitated and anxious all the time.

So, balance your activities, go deep within, and you will perceive that you lack the nurturing and comforting "spiritual bread."

Reorganize your life and restore balance to it while there is still time.

CIII

Take a good look at how much time you dedicate to your spiritual life every day.

You go to work, get dressed, entertain yourself, eat, sleep and devote a few minutes to your incarnate Spirit by way of a short prayer or a brief reading, or you listen to a lecture. But maybe sometimes you do none of these.

Humans are not just mind and body. Above and foremost they are spirits that command the mind-body components. As such, they require spiritual sustenance to properly perform their tasks.

The body needs upkeep to live, but so does the soul.

CIV

Envy is a mighty, inner foe that you must overcome.

It viciously infiltrates your mental screens and wreaks havoc on your emotions.

It becomes a ruthless inspector, an insensitive taskmaster.

It sets up traps; it seeks revenge through thought, word and deed; it persecutes implacably.

Countless crimes were born out of envy, not including those that never actually materialize.

Envy is a feeling of inferiority that must be rectified and transformed into camaraderie and contentment.

Joanna de Ângelis/Divaldo Franco

CV

Don't make space in your mind for vulgar thoughts.

Fill every gap with uplifting ideas, activities for the good, and plans for your own and your neighbor's happiness.

Action plans begin in the mind.

The idle mind creates regrettable images that materialize with great destructive power, consuming the one who pictures them and striking others.

Fight consciously so that your *empty hours* are not filled with mental garbage, making you unhappy or vulgar.

CVI

Sadness is suffering's courier.

Do not hold on to sadness or let it contaminate you with its miasmas.

Of course, not every day is bright and rich with joy.

At times, suffering seems to gain the upper hand. When this happens, analyze the problem, sense the pain, and make your inner sun shine, driving away the sadness. In so doing, you will more easily overcome life's trials.

Cultivating sadness renders you vulnerable to mental, emotional and physical infirmities.

CVII

Be sensible always.

You are better off losing something in an argument than becoming embroiled in a battle that will cause you greater harm.

It is not about fear but wisdom.

Peaceable individuals are happy; trifles cannot upset them.

It is a matter of choice. Which is better: winning an argument so as not to seem ignorant or foolish, or *losing* it in the name of prudence and wisdom?

Good sense always prevails. What it does not win on the outside, it gains as inner peace.

CVIII

Be a friend to all who seek your company and support.

People need friends as much as they need bread to live.

Amidst the crowd there are many lonely hearts in need of companionship and friendship.

Never say goodbye to anyone without offering something of value from the time you have spent together.

You have much to give. Finding out your qualities is the first step. Using them on behalf of others is the next.

No one is so lacking in spiritual resources that they have nothing at all to give.

CIX

Don't vent your anger at those around you on account of your frustrations and complexes.

They suffer enough already without having to deal with your load of bitterness and problems.

Trade places with them and you will see how much you would appreciate a little kindness and compassion to mitigate your humiliation and suffering.

They are your needy brothers and sisters.

Should they be scornful and rude, teach them with silence and benevolence.

They are unacquainted with good manners, so they need your example.

CX

Give those who have wronged you a second chance, facilitating reconciliation.

Be receptive.

They could have changed their mind and realized their error, and are now waiting for a chance.

We all make mistakes and hope for an opportunity to make things right.

If you close yourself off in your pain and want nothing more to do with them, your attitude is just as bad if not worse than theirs.

Do not let your wounded pride rob you of an excellent opportunity for a triumph over yourself.

CXI

Examine your conscience as often as possible.

If you were to take a closer look at your behavior, many complaints and grievances would disappear.

We readily spot other people's problems and mistakes.

Usually, when others create difficulties and put up obstacles, they do so in reaction to your behavior – the way you have expressed yourself and the way you have acted.

Have the courage to examine yourself more severely, calling to mind attitudes and words. Upon discovering mistakes, correct them right away. Seek out those whom you have upset and make amends.

Do not persevere in error, whatever the reason.

CXII

Read something comforting and inspiring every day, however brief.

Make it a habit.

It will enrich you with joy, dispersing the dark clouds that may envelop you afterwards, and providing you with well-being should something unpleasant come up.

Everyone needs a good counselor, and in the pages of the Gospel you will find sure guidelines and words of wisdom for every occasion.

If people would only think before acting, they would avert countless evils.

Be one who does, even if others do not.

CXIII

Never lose hope.

Trust always, come what may.

If all conspires against you and failure has you at the brink of despair, continue to expect Divine Aid even so.

The only thing that happens to us is what is best for us.

The law of God is love. With love, all things are possible.

When you think help may arrive too late, hold steady and you will discover that it did arrive and just in the nick of time.

People who despair have already lost part of the battle.

CXIV

The youthfulness of your body is short-lived.

Use it to store up eternal values.

The prime of life passes quickly, but our preset commitments extend over an entire lifetime.

Be mindful of them.

Good commitments will be like watchful sentinels along the way, blessing the hours; bad ones will be like ruthless creditors, perturbing your peace.

Place signs of light along your path, marking the ground you have gained.

Remain young at every age by way of upright conduct and a conscience free of regrets.

CXV

Discipline your will so as not to succumb to irresponsibility.

Start small, maintaining order and efficiency in each endeavor.

When you have a lot to do, don't waste time deciding how to begin.

Start with the closest task and then move on to the next, and so on until you have finished them all.

Unless you take the first step, you will never reach the end.

A lecture begins with the first word.

Discipline is behind the success of all great achievements.

CXVI

Of course, you cannot solve all of the world's problems.

However, you can and must make your contribution.

While you cannot put an end to war, you have resources to avert personal disputes. While you cannot feed the starving multitudes, you can offer one person a slice of bread. While you cannot offer health to all the infirm, you can help one sick person. While you cannot avert human tragedies, you can comfort someone in distress. While you cannot mobilize the masses to speed up the changes the world needs, you can change yourself inwardly, ennobling yourself in working for the Good and solidarity.

CXVII

In the midst of your responsibilities, set aside some time for beauty.

Get up early to witness the dawn, inebriating yourself with the strength of the light.

Walk in silence through the woods and breathe the fresh air.

Walk along a deserted beach and reflect on the majesty of the sea.

Gaze at the stars and ask silent questions.

Observe a rose in full bloom...

Linger next to an innocent child...

Talk with a senior citizen...

Open up to the beauty in everything and adorn yourself with it.

CXVIII

Accept people as they are.

This arrogant, disagreeable person is sick and probably does not know it.

That intractable colleague is unhappy on the inside.

That demanding acquaintance over there has frazzled nerves.

Some, those who seem prideful, are merely trying to hide their conflicts.

Others, those who appear indifferent, have terrible fears.

The earth is a massive hospital for souls.

Those who see you only on the surface have no way of really knowing you.

Grant people the freedom to be who they are, and not who you expect them to be.

CXIX

Be wise by investing in your future.

What happens to you today results from a past you can no longer change.

But what happens tomorrow will result from the choices you make today.

While you harvest the effects of past actions, you are also acting for future consequences.

You reap what you sow.

The Good is your destiny. How you get there is up to you. You can get there quickly, or you can get there slowly with multiple stops along the way.

No one is destined to suffer. Suffering is the product of bad choices.

Invest in tomorrow and you will be happy, starting today.

CXX

Even if you do not know it, you are somebody's role model.

There is always someone watching what you do, tuning into it even if it is wrong.

For that reason, you are responsible not only for what you do, but also for how your ideas and attitudes inspire others.

Dictators and tyrants by themselves could not do much were it not for those who think like them and support them.

Likewise, the work of the Good would fail were it not for those who are selflessly and lovingly connected with it.

Be aware of your words and deeds, stimulating followers who will grow spiritually and act correctly.

CXXI

Listen calmly whenever you are asked to.

Allow the other person to finish his or her thought, without jumping to conclusions, which are almost always incorrect.

Few can express themselves quickly and clearly.

So, listen good-naturedly, overlooking inappropriate expressions, sincerely trying to understand what he or she wishes to say.

If you are being blamed for something, find the root of the problem and pull it out. Dialogue should always be cordial, leaving a positive balance.

If you are being instructed, assimilate the lesson.

If a third party is being accused, lessen the intensity of the rebuke with expressions of comfort.

Joanna de Ângelis/Divaldo Franco

CXXII

Be yourself regardless of the circumstances.

Don't try to come across as superior or inferior to what you really are.

If you want a better position, work hard to get it.

Whenever you find imperfections, strive to improve yourself.

People lie either when they purport to have skills they do not actually have, or when they hide or deny the ones they do have.

Being genuine is a way to acquire dignity.

The ascent is slow for everyone.

Those succeeding today began their struggle earlier on.

Those struggling at present will succeed at a later time.

Don't be self-conscious on account of your trials.

Your friends have walked, in their time, the same path you tread today.

CXXIII

Your work, seemingly demeaning and disdained by others, is your treasure, a tool for you to earn your keep and bring you honor.

Perform your task mindfully and honorably.

The shining diamond came from the entrails of the earth, where it kept company with worms, and the delicious bread gracing your table came from wheat that grew in the dirt…

Working is a challenge for everybody.

As long as humankind continues to produce, the march of progress continues uninterrupted.

Honor your labor by being its faithful servant.

CXXIV

Spite is responsible for many evils.

It is a *weed* that takes root in the sickness of envy.

Spite breeds unwarranted persecutions, never-ending accusations and toxic gossip.

Spiteful persons cannot forgive another person's success.

They always find the negative side of every issue – "the needle in the haystack."

They suffer needlessly, are ever bitter, and fight the dragons they see in others when, in reality, the problem is theirs alone.

Learn to celebrate other people's achievements and you will transcend spite.

Joanna de Ângelis/Divaldo Franco

CXXV

Continue to study and learn.

Make good reading part of your activities. One page per day, a small passage during breaks at work, a sentence to meditate on – all become a strong foundation for your future.

Knowledge is an asset which, no matter how much you store up, never takes up any space. Much to the contrary, it broadens your horizons.

Good reading enriches the mind, soothes the heart and stimulates progress.

An ignorant person fumbles around in the dark.

Read a little at a time, but do it consistently.

CXXVI

A bit of inner silence will do you a lot of good.

The constant hustle and bustle, endless worries and the unexpected all diminish one's moral endurance. It is imperative to set aside some time to recover and practice inner silence.

Pray silently, calmly; let your ideas flow spontaneously, recomposing your emotional and nerve pathways so that you may rejoin the struggle.

During such times, reconnect with yourself and experience the joy of loving, caring for and renewing yourself so that no traces of negativity remain.

CXXVII

Don't spoil your day by internalizing insults.

Of course there are people who do not like you and even detest you. This should come as no surprise, for you feel the same way in relation to others.

Peaceable hearts easily solve this problem because they never take offenses seriously.

Many kind and affable persons surround you, so it is pointless for you to become aggravated with those who prove to be one of the exceptions.

Cast the offense into the dust of oblivion and proceed in the direction of the love that awaits you.

CXXVIII

There is a sun shining within you. It is Christ's presence in your heart.

Don't cloud it over with a bad mood, rebelliousness or discontent …

An outside light source does shine, but it casts a shadow upon encountering an obstacle.

Your inner sun never casts one, because it gives off light from the inside out, in abundance.

With love as its fuel, your light will shine ever brighter, radiating its blessing in all directions.

May your light shine far and wide.

Joanna de Ângelis/Divaldo Franco

CXXIX

There is still time to correct a regrettable situation currently receding into the past.

While you are still on the road with the other person, there is a chance for a do-over and making amends.

If he or she is unwilling, it is no longer your problem.

However, until you do decide to do so, you remain in debt.

Misunderstandings happen all the time. Keeping them alive is a choice, the result of human pride.

Clear your head with the superior attitude of letting go of emotional garbage, seeking out those you have wronged so that you may rectify the situation.

CXXX

Being on time is not only a duty but also a sign of respect and honor for those waiting or relying on you.

If you plan carefully, you will rarely be late.

The habit of being on time is forged in the same way as the habit of being late.

Schedule your commitments and calmly fulfill each, one by one.

In the event that you cannot make it at all, or if you have to be late, communicate it ahead of time to free the other person from the commitment.

That way, should something come up and you have to be late, then even if your explanation is not believed, you will be at peace.

Joanna de Ângelis/Divaldo Franco

CXXXI

When you are facing difficulties and tough trials on the road of spiritual growth, seek shelter in a heartfelt prayer of faith in God. It will keep you from falling into the abyss of rebelliousness.

A bit of inner silence and concentration, the soul locked in prayer and open to inspiration: these are necessary for you to receive the reassuring Divine Response.

Make the climate of prayer a habit and you will be in perennial communion with God, strengthened for the challenges ahead.

CXXXII

The natural events of human existence are seen as misfortunes: the loss of loved ones, accidents with long-term effects, financial ruin, emotional downfalls, earthquakes and other calamities…

While they are clearly serious problems, they do not qualify as real disasters, except for those who allow themselves to be upended by their effects, wiping out life's higher objectives.

When we know how to deal with these setbacks, we can benefit enormously from them.

Joanna de Ângelis/Divaldo Franco

CXXXIII

The opportunities for moral ascent that life affords you must be seized readily and wisely.

Time marches on inexorably, and an overlooked chance is lost for good.

Once time and wind pass, they never return.

Thus, taking advantage of every opportunity for inner growth is a blessing that will set you free.

Stay vigilant so as to put all your time to good use.

CXXXIV

Repeat an error-filled lesson gladly.

The learning process employs various techniques to impart knowledge. "Trial and error" is the most common one.

The same is true for moral lessons.

If corrected by repeating the experience, today's error becomes a lesson that will endure forever.

Joanna de Ângelis/Divaldo Franco

CXXXV

While you have the resources, cultivate solidarity.

You are a social being who needs to coexist with other people in order to fulfill the goals for which you were reborn.

Solidarity is one of the most valuable tools for success.

Be useful and kind; spread goodness, and in return, you will never be lonely.

CXXXVI

Be tolerant toward your neighbor in the measure that you would expect to receive it.

On today's earth there is no one whose journey is without error, fear and torment. These cause affliction when you are trying to do what is right and they cause suffering when your are trying to appease, requiring understanding and tolerance.

For that reason, sow tolerance today in order to reap it tomorrow.

Joanna de Ângelis/Divaldo Franco

CXXXVII

Despite your affective and social relations, the trials that enable you to evolve never come as a surprise. They hinge on you alone.

Loved ones, friends and colleagues may share in your pain, but the cross you bear will always be personal.

It could not be otherwise.

Under the loving gaze of Divine Justice, people's expiations are in conformance with their own debts. Individuals grow according to the circumstances in which they erred.

Equip yourself with peace and faith in preparation for the unavoidable ascent required of you.

CXXXVIII

Be a suitable friend, knowing how to act discreetly and uprightly toward those who have chosen your friendship.

Discretion is a treasure seldom practiced in friendships on the earth. It is usually replaced by senselessness and superficiality.

Everyone enjoys dignified and virtuous company, the kind that inspires trust and fosters well-being.

Listen, watch, accompany and converse with decorum, honoring the trust bestowed upon you.

Joanna de Ângelis/Divaldo Franco

CXXXIX

Some people use truth as a weapon to attack others.

Truth, however, reflects a magnificent light that promotes understanding, which never harms or hurts.

Like bread, it must be ingested in proper amounts; or like water, which should be drunk in the right amount.

As truth nourishes and quenches, it appeases and satisfies, enriching those whom it penetrates with understanding and kindness.

Never use it harshly as a weapon to destroy others; otherwise, it loses its purpose: setting one free.

CXL

Never tire of loving.

You may see no immediate results.

You may be taken aback by people's reactions. It is even possible that the outcome may be downright depressing.

Unaccustomed to pure sentiments, people react to them with self-defense mechanisms.

If you persist, however, you will prove the excellence of that boundless sentiment and you will connect with those you love, receiving back love's inherent blessings.

Therefore, love always.

CXLI

Measure your emotions carefully.

Pretentiousness is always unpleasant, just as unjustifiable aloofness is to blame for many problems in social relations.

Pretentiousness is a behavioral disorder, just as aloofness is a symptom of insecurity.

Analyze yourself lovingly and sincerely, looking to overcome the fears and anxieties responsible for your behavior.

A calm attitude is a sign of self-realization, which you will achieve only through prayer, patience and meditation.

In so doing, emotional control is feasible.

CXLII

Your real needs will never exceed your means.

Each person is born or reborn into the circumstances best suited for happiness.

Discontent and rebelliousness, however, usually arm people with ambition and aggressiveness, generating unfortunate states, despite their having accumulated excesses and trinkets, to which they attribute too much worth.

If only the human heart were not dominated by selfishness, greed and indifference, no one would ever want for the essentials.

CXLIII

Be a friend of truth, never using it as a weapon of destruction or offense.

It is not so much what you say but how you say it that produces good or bad results.

Besides, yours may not be the real truth, but only a reflection of it. Even if it were the real truth, you have no right to brandish it for perturbing purposes.

Before you assume the role of someone who corrects and teaches with the truth, put yourself in the other person's shoes and your conscience will guide you in relation to the best way to proceed and express yourself.

CXLIV

Always make the decision that will produce the least harm for yourself and others.

Before assuming commitments, ponder the possible results and you will more easily know how to choose those that are best for your future.

Whenever your gain might be someone else's loss, reject it, for no one can be happy raising his or her joy over the misfortune of others.

In other words, "Do not do unto others what you would not have them do unto you."

Whatever you lose today to someone else, you will receive tomorrow without harming anyone.

CXLV

You do not observe life from a distance.

You are a member of the universal community, endowed with tasks and responsibilities whose fulfillment by you will result in the order and success of many things.

Taking the posture of an outside observer leads to erroneous approaches and conclusions. Only conscious participation makes for the correct approach and the correct interpretation of the data at hand.

Consider yourself a valuable element in the whole of creation. Each day, become more active in the Father's Vineyard, making it better known and appreciated.

You are God's heir, and the universe, in a sense, belongs to you.

Happy Life

CXLVI

Irritability is a *thorn* deeply imbedded in the *flesh* of the emotions. It needs to be extracted.

The longer it remains in place, the greater the damage, causing harmful and long lasting *infections*.

Irritable people do not need reasons for moodiness or discontentment. It is easy for them to channel their germs into aggressiveness and bitterness.

These individuals become unbearable, giving off the morbid energy that characterizes their behavior.

They feel good when they aggravate others and rejoice when they get revenge on someone who offended them, even if it was done unintentionally.

They enjoy being unhappy.

Overcome irritation or it will destroy you.

CXLVII

If one of your projects has failed, don't get upset or give up.

Apparent failures are the means by which God teaches you to correct your approach, enabling you to repeat the experience all the wiser.

A person who refuses to try again on account of a past failure doesn't deserve to enjoy the sweet taste of success.

The art of starting over is the measure of greatness for those who aspire to even greater accomplishments.

No one enjoys victory without having experienced previous defeats.

Life is a succession of lessons that must be repeated until properly learned.

Joanna de Ângelis/Divaldo Franco

CXLVIII

Everyone suffers while in the world.

Pain is an effective tool for renewal when the benefits of unfulfilled love die.

In light of this unavoidable fact, pain – which the Spirit confronts in its myriad modalities – must be accepted with dignity and trust.

What today seems tormenting and threatening will become peace tomorrow.

Physical and mental illness, financial or mental distress will pass, leaving results in proportion to the degree of personal maturity with which they were endured.

So, don't feel sorry for yourself when you suffer. Reap the benefits and courageously press on.

CXLIX

God knows your destiny and is in control of your life.

You deserve whatever happens to you so that you may gain new ground along the evolutionary continuum.

God is a Merciful Father who watches over you.

Never consider yourself overlooked, tumbling down the slippery slope of rebelliousness and blasphemy.

Humans must practice courage and resignation; otherwise they will stay spiritually immature.

God does not play favorites. God loves everyone the same way.

Joanna de Ângelis/Divaldo Franco

Let yourself be led by events you cannot change, while lovingly changing those that will benefit you.

Falling into despair? Never!

CL

Abandon your plans for revenge in relation to mean, selfish, upsetting or disrespectful people.

There are still those who delight in wrongdoing, who aggravate and boast about it.

These people are barely out of the primitive stages, slowly acquiring the light of reason and the sensibility of emotion.

It would not be right to stoop to their level, suffering even more, when you could rise to a higher level and lift them up, thus improving the world's moral landscape.

Be the one to promote growth and understanding in relation to your neighbor's shortcomings.

You will never regret acting this way.

Joanna de Ângelis/Divaldo Franco

CLI

Be wary of immoral fantasies. They pervert both your emotions and your sexuality!

They become engrained on your mental screens and create afflictive cravings that torment and destabilize you.

What you cultivate in your imagination can become an angel of assistance, if noble, or a demon when vulgar.

In the physical arena there are serious moral behaviors that are sustained by maddening mental passions.

Think and act harmoniously.

Cultivate uplifting ideas and you will be blissful.

CLII

Calm the anxieties of your heart.

What you have not yet attained is on the way.

Do not suffer in anticipation by giving in to depression because you lack what you do not even need.

Scarcity can provide appreciation for people and things.

Abundance often does the opposite.

Learn to coexist with scarcity and solitude and you will avoid the intoxication of the senses, the ecstasy of lust and the headaches of ownership.

You are what you make of yourself and not what you possess or whom you are with.

Joanna de Ângelis/Divaldo Franco

CLIII

Give yourself the right to remain impassive when provoked.

In this insensitive day and age, evil runs rampant, seducing the heedless.

Here, the anger of those who attack you.

There, unbridled sex tempts you.

Over there, ambition awakens your interests.

Vice closes in, ensnaring its victims.

All around you, troubling forms of entertainment are rife.

Everywhere, the triumph of crime and the disintegration of values spread their tentacles like a cruel and domineering octopus.

See such *features* as a trail of poisonous thorns hidden under lush, green grass. Do not step there, thus avoiding grave harm.

Happy Life

CLIV

The moment you make high-minded resolutions and spare yourself mental imbalance, people will try to convince you that you are making a big mistake.

Stay the course and don't listen to them.

When you fall, few hands will try to help you up.

There is no lack of those who will push you even deeper into the abyss of despair.

Sadly, selfless helpers are in the minority, while the majority love to cause you grief.

Continue on the path of goodness, and the Good will be very good to you.

Joanna de Ângelis/Divaldo Franco

CLV

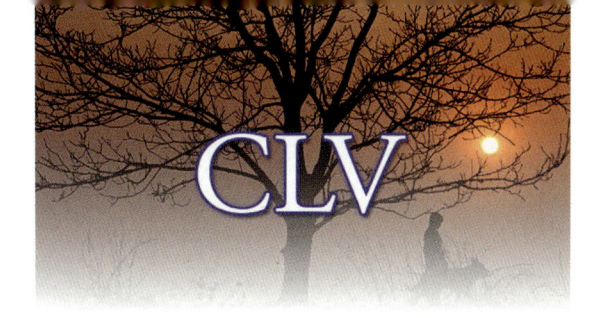

Learn from life's lessons but, more importantly, learn from your own experiences. Be wary of the *siren song*, which can lure you onto the reef.

When alcoholics wish to stop drinking, it is easier for them to find someone willing to serve them another drink than someone to give them bread.

When smokers want to stop smoking, they are met with the sarcasm of their friends who insist they continue poisoning themselves.

When drug addicts want to stop using, dealers threaten and blackmail them.

When offenders of any kind attempt rehabilitation, a conspiring mob pushes back.

So be careful. Stay physically and morally sound.

CLVI

Make it a habit to tell the truth.

The white lie habit is a gateway to more serious ones, pushing you toward the quagmire of libel and slander.

A single spark produces the same blaze as a crackling flame.

Major crimes begin as misdemeanors overlooked by Justice, which make for a more severe offence.

Be morally demanding of yourself. Don't climb into the boat of general conventions.

Every person must answer for him or herself and each deed leaves a mark on the conscience.

Don't stop being yourself as you morally progress.

CLVII

Illuminate yourself with prayer as often as possible.

Create a mental space and tap into the Springs of Life, where you can absorb pure energies and peace.

All the saints and mystics who have altered the course of humankind for the better in the East and the West have unanimously pointed to prayer as the most effective tool for both achieving and preserving inner harmony.

Jesus cheerfully spent much time with His disciples and the masses; however, He also reserved time to talk with God through prayer and He praised the excellence of such sublime colloquies for others.

So, leave the turmoil for the oasis of prayer to bask in self-renewal and peace.

Joanna de Ângelis/Divaldo Franco

CLVIII

Ill-gotten gains are pure poison.

Many rave about and justify their huge profit margins, saying that they are consistent with the times and that everyone should take advantage of them.

Since such morality is corrupt, don't let it guide you. Instead, control the abuses and excesses that come to your attention so that you may correct the chaotic situation.

Wrongdoing should never be used as an example to follow.

During flu season, the flu does not become the normal state of health simply because most people come down with it.

Immunize yourself against abuses and you will lead an orderly life – perhaps without the superfluous, but never in want of the essentials.

CLIX

The moment people resolve to modify their moral behavior for the better, they seem to encounter a general conspiracy against them.

Everything changes and spins out of control.

Minor things become complicated and the course of events takes a turn for the worse for a while.

As a result, they give up.

However, this is all natural.

Every change must break with what has been the norm.

In the moral arena, the reaction is even greater, because it reaches down to the root of evil in order to pull it out so that balanced behavior may grow in its place.

So, do not give up on your plans for moral renewal and inner growth by virtue of the initial challenges.

CLX

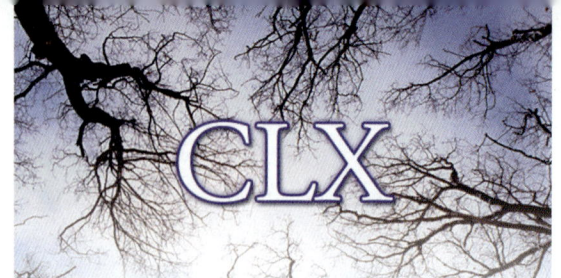

In a 24-hour day, set aside a few moments for reflection.

Those who do not meditate lose touch with themselves.

Bound to the hands of the clock, either way ahead of time or far behind, people get overwhelmed and lose direction.

Success demands periodic reassessment of one's goals and actions.

Reflection allows you to identify mistakes and correct them in time, to reformulate your responsibilities and renew yourself more easily.

Speak and sleep a little less; meditate a little more.

If you use wasted minutes in order to meditate, they will become points of light during your day.

Joanna de Angelis/Divaldo Franco

CLXI

We are all destined for happiness and perfection.

It is a long journey, sometimes marked with thorns or strewn with stones.

Nevertheless, the course is the same for all. There are no exceptions.

People having to face fewer difficulties are reaping the rewards of their behavior in past reincarnations.

Likewise, people dealing with many difficulties are suffering from unfortunate deeds.

So, gain evolutionary ground step by step, and rejoice over the blissful destination awaiting you. You are sure to reach it.

CLXII

Be careful with friends whose hearts have grown cold.

Some people have killed their emotions and have become indifferent to the Good. They give off toxic miasmas and are bearers of maleficent pessimism that brings down everybody around them.

Therefore, widen your circle of friends but be wary of these perturbing and discouraging influences.

Such bitter people merely drift about, casting their dark shadow everywhere they go.

Let the sun shine on you.

CLXIII

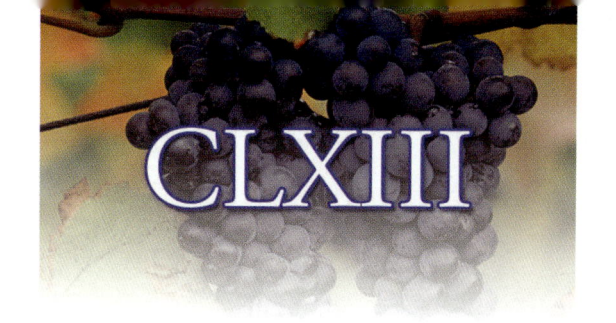

Keep searching for your true identity, that is, discover yourself for your own good.

You will see that you're neither better nor worse than others. What counts is what you make of yourself.

With this awareness you will realize that you have no right to special privileges, nor has God abandoned you.

Transform all that happens to you into a valuable lesson for your spiritual growth. That is why you are on the earth.

Gather up all your triumphs and make them lessons of wisdom that will enrich you with blessings.

CLXIV

Many anguish over the wrongs that other people can inflict on them.

They project responsibility for their failures onto others and they see enemies everywhere. This is a maneuver to escape the need for self-examination.

They wander the paths of wrongdoings and accusations.

With such a mindset, they hurt, harm and disturb others and do not realize the evil they have carelessly surrendered to.

It is the badness that resides within individuals that makes them bad, turning them into pernicious elements in the social fabric.

CLXV

Cleanse your organism with positive thoughts.

The power of the mind over the emotions, the body and the entire physiological machinery is incontestable.

Many infirmities originate in mental idleness, depression, rebelliousness or self--destructive thoughts.

Channel your thinking toward pleasant, wholesome and optimistic ideas. You will benefit from it, enjoying well-being that will radiate outward to others, bringing about peace.

CLXVI

Your importance is in direct proportion to the good that you do on your own behalf.

With or without you, life goes on and the world keeps on turning.

Don't think that you are a bearer of exceptional characteristics, without which others would perish and humanity would come undone.

Your wins and losses give an account of your real values.

Practice simplicity and strive for humility, like a light bulb compared to the sun and the sun compared to the galaxy…

Joanna de Ângelis/Divaldo Franco

CLXVII

People's greatness can be measured by their capacity for service, humility and love.

Big people stand out and cast a shadow, whereas great people become inextinguishable points of light, showing the way to freedom.

True heroes ignore themselves. They are more concerned with helping others rather than advertising their own deeds.

Be like them in the silence of your accomplishments and the greatness of your smallness.

CLXVIII

Surreptitiously, intrigue sneaks its way into your heart, closing the door of your sentiments to serenity.

You turn cold and calculating, heartless and defensive toward others, who perhaps do not deserve this reaction from you.

Intriguers always find a way to poison you.

Knowing your temperament, they subtly infiltrate your defenses, injecting you with toxic information.

Fight back against intrigue and educate intriguers so that they will leave you in peace and have peace themselves, thereby changing their mindset and their morals.

CLXIX

Attend a funeral occasionally in order to delve more deeply into the biological phenomena of life and death.

By observing that death happens to others, you will awaken to what will inevitably happen to you.

The spirit is eternal, while the life of the body is brief and transitory.

Right now you feel that all is fine and that it will remain so for a long time. But how long will that last, really? What is your guarantee in relation to your time on earth?

So, live well but do not discard the possibility of your departure, which, incidentally, is the only certainty.

CLXX

Stay calm in every situation.

Many live in permanent despair and self-consuming haste.

They bump into one another in a frenzy, without enjoying what they have already accomplished or amassed.

Serenity and well-being go hand in hand, for serenity fosters the pleasure that blesses and fulfills.

Come back into harmony, calmly manage the passing of the hours and live with the serene joy of being on the earth and being able to advance toward God, our ultimate goal.

Joanna de Ângelis/Divaldo Franco

CLXXI

Control your will, generating a climate of discipline for your habits, and you will avert unruliness, behavioral issues and disagreements.

People who do not believe in discipline are like a person driving a car going downhill without brakes... They are candidates for disaster.

What you give life to through thought materializes in the world of forms.

By learning to discern and struggle for what is best, you will learn to conduct yourself appropriately. It will spare you innumerable aggravations.

A well-directed will accomplishes great things.

So, channel it wisely and you will never regret it.

Happy Life

CLXXII

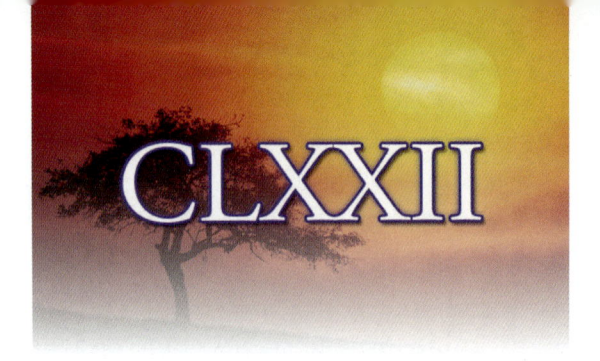

The acquisition of knowledge is a personal, non-transferrable accomplishment.

It is a treasure that grows when it is shared and no one can steal it.

Not even death can claim it, for knowledge crosses over with the Spirit as an asset of constant worth and of easy access.

Strive to acquire knowledge; it's never too late. Increase what knowledge you already have or start acquiring it now if you have yet to experience the pleasure it brings.

Knowledgeable people are more confident and circumvent countless setbacks.

Conversely, ignorance is responsible for countless problems.

Joanna de Ângelis/Divaldo Franco

CLXXIII

Be kind and gracious, generating affinity and friendship.

Don't delegate what you yourself can handle.

You have no right to overload those who work with you, demanding what lies beyond their possibilities.

Even your employees deserve your consideration and respect. They work for you and get paid.

But do more: make them your friends.

There are small, tedious tasks assigned to them that you yourself could handle without tiring yourself out or belittling your employees.

In your relationship with them, use "please" and "thank you," thereby teaching them to be more polite and spreading affection around you.

CLXXIV

True courage shows in the way we face life's daily battles.

Courage should not be confused with recklessness.

Courage is calm, persevering, lucid and creative, whereas recklessness is desperate, aggressive and irritable.

Courage is born of faith that knows what it wants and strives to achieve it. It is undiminished when facing obstacles and does not lose its strength through time. It thinks before acting and draws illumination from the ideal when on the battlefield.

Show your courage through balanced, correct action.

CLXXV

Keep quiet about what you hear.

People would spare themselves a lot of heartaches if they knew how to listen and reflect.

Unfortunately, many rush to spread the news, altering its content and stressing the sensitive or negative points.

Fragmented accounts and adulterated stories have the *magical power* to disturb, creating conflicts and unbearable situations.

Don't spread toxic information.

Listen calmly without jumping to conclusions.

If you wish to comment, do so benignly and as if you were the one involved in the situation.

CLXXVI

Keep your personal style clean and simple.

Humility is often mistaken with slovenliness, opening the door to inexcusable untidiness.

Likewise, it is wrongly assumed that a good appearance implies conceited refinement or fashion.

The Scriptures state that "Jesus' garments became as white as the light," attesting to His purity and power, reflected in His clothes.

He never got sick and He never appeared in public wearing distasteful or bizarre clothing.

Like His friends, He wore the clothing of the time, although He endowed it with His mighty glow.

Your own magnetism will shine through, enhancing or diminishing your appearance, which deserves your proper care.

CLXXVII

Allow people to finish what they are saying without interrupting. Of course, there is a limit to this. However, if you listen, you will be better prepared to enlighten them.

If you interrupt, you might reach the wrong conclusion and miss out on what they are trying to tell you.

Not everyone can express themselves easily and they sometimes go in circles or are unclear.

Seek to grasp the main idea and dialogue without impatience or exasperation.

Don't impose your thoughts or try to stop others from voicing ideas different than your own.

Happy Life

CLXXVIII

Control your anxiety.

Unchecked anxiety causes all kinds of physical damage and generates unease wherever it appears.

It radiates a disturbing wave and spreads insecurity all around.

Anxious people require more attention, which is not always available. They are always complaining and causing problems for others. They see things that are not even happening, and they rush into undesirable situations only to regret it later.

Serenity is anxiety's blessed antidote. It appears the moment you choose to strive to live in peace and trust in God.

CLXXIX

Coveting other people's assets is a widespread evil.

Slowly, people grow dissatisfied, coveting what does not belong to them or what they do not really need.

If only everyone were satisfied with what they have, life would be richer with beauty and experience.

There is a widely spread false idea of happiness nowadays known as "keeping up with the Joneses."

Everybody wants what their neighbor has, and the imitation of fantasies and chimeras produced by their imagination has become their goal.

Those who cannot keep up with the Joneses feel rejected, unhappy.

Don't covet anything anybody has.

Seek self-realization and enjoy peace.

CLXXX

Let the light of your faith shine through your smile, your words and your attitude toward life.

The world needs light to overcome the prevailing darkness.

Expand your confident, luminous presence, helping the shy, the disheartened, the fallen and the rebellious.

Light always attracts, enriching with beauty.

Don't let that star go out on account of the surrounding antagonistic elements.

Let it shine, pointing out blessed pathways for those longing for a chance at self-realization.

Happy Life

CLXXXI

Love is life's greatest lesson.

Without love, goals have no meaning, leaving people at the mercy of their lower passions.

Love disperses negativity's shadows and infuses gentleness into every act.

Therefore, love everyone and everything.

Practice loving nature, resplendent in the sun, air, water, trees, flowers, fruits, animals and human beings.

Let yourself be moved by the silent invitations that the Divine Father extends to you, and pour out your emotions on all things, softening yourself on the inside.

Joanna de Ângelis/Divaldo Franco

The more you love, the less the claws of evil will reach you, for your heightened awareness will broaden your connection with life, and you will harvest only the effects of peace.

CLXXXII

When a person opts for an upright life, a relentless inner struggle ensues.

Like two armies clashing on the mental battlefield, non-stop confrontations rage on.

The usual warriors – selfishness, pride, violence and ambition – try to defeat the new combatants – love for one's neighbor, humility, peace and selflessness.

The person feels anguished and torn.

The light of Divine Inspiration, however, shines on this stark battlefield, enlightening the soul and encouraging it to persist in its higher purposes.

Invest your best efforts in life's battles and don't surrender.

Each day of resistance is a battle won, drawing you closer to final victory.

Joanna de Ângelis/Divaldo Franco

CLXXXIII

Be sincerely forgiving in relation to widespread ignorance.

Don't expect an apology from your transgressor.

Move past the hard-to-digest ingredients of aggression and stay balanced, seeking to really forget the regrettable incident.

Those who harbor resentment poison themselves with the miasmas they emit.

Assailants are seriously ill and need the balm of benevolence to heal.

Having lost their mental clarity, they attack.

Grant them the chance they deny you.

Being benevolent is always the more comfortable position.

So, you be the giver, signifying that you have already achieved what the other person still lacks.

CLXXXIV

At your workplace you may encounter conspirators against your peace-of-mind.

The world is a broad arena where the improvident choose to fight one another rather than love one another.

In some cases, they become unconscious *beasts* that merely react, always assuming attitudes that are improper for their station in life, seeking to take the place of others, to bring them down, to see them suffer.

Avoid this criminal and maddening competition; act uprightly and conscientiously.

What is yours, no one can take, and no amount of slander will veil your merit.

Therefore, act rightly and hold on to your peace-of-mind.

CLXXXV

Sooner or later, suffering will reach your heart, for it is an integral component of life in progress.

Without suffering, arrogance, despotism and violence would become unbearable.

Since humans still don't listen to the soft voice of love, affliction smooths out their rough edges and persuades them to reflect, to pursue the Good.

At times people react, blaspheme, kick and scream, but finally surrender, which is the only way to break free.

So, don't rebel in the face of suffering. It will make your predicament even worse and you will wear yourself out needlessly.

Active acceptance, i.e., the conversion of suffering into experience, is what brings about the *miracle* of success.

Joanna de Ângelis/Divaldo Franco

CLXXXVI

The home is the family's temple.

Children are Divine Loans for building a blissful future.

One should spend as much time as possible with the family, using conversation and setting good examples, making family time the most effective tool for education.

The habits acquired in the home last throughout one's life and cross over into the spirit life.

To educate is to live with dignity, imprinting family members with life's essential values.

Everything you invest in the home will return in kind.

Make your home life a workshop where happiness dwells.

CLXXXVII

In today's stressful times, anguish – disguised as fear, anxiety and guilt – is people's constant companion.

Clearly, this is due to the many pressures to which they are subjected.

The anxiety for exorbitant pleasures produces frustration, violence breeds fear, and timidity sets the dynamics for self-punishment in motion.

Such phantasms are responsible for countless ills. Remove them from you mind.

You are God's child. He loves, protects and blesses you.

Don't stray from His laws, and should you lose your way, fearlessly return to the pathway of duty instead of surrendering to unnecessary turmoil.

Joanna de Ângelis/Divaldo Franco

CLXXXVIII

Never pass up on an opportunity to be helpful.

It is not just with money, an important social position, or personal influence that you can help.

A kind word provides encouragement and works wonders.

Words have built civilizations as much as they have led people into war and destruction.

Use words to help, motivating the fallen to get back up, those who sleep to wake up, the mistaken to make amends, and the violent to calm down.

Speak kindly and loftily, becoming a loyal microphone in the service of the Good.

CLXXXIX

Your life does not end at the grave.

With that in mind, learn in preparation for eternity, storing up everlasting values.

Every lesson that delivers one from evil is incorporated into the soul as an indestructible life force.

Were death the end of life, the universe would not make sense.

Creation would come to an end and thinking beings would have no purpose.

However, everything calls humans to eternal glory, the continuation of life and unending progress.

Study and work incessantly, with your sights set on your spiritual future, living blissfully today and fulfilled always.

Joanna de Ângelis/Divaldo Franco

CXC

Problems are challenges.

All thinking beings face problems, for life in the physical body unfolds amid a myriad of difficult situations.

Learn to live with problems while trying to solve them on your own as far as possible. When this is not possible, turn to someone with experience and work hard until reaching a resolution.

Don't put your problems on others; they have their own, even though they may not show it.

It would be inconsiderate to burden others with our problems, disregarding the afflictions that surely weigh them down.

A problem solved today is a lesson for solving future ones.

Learn how to solve them so you may live in peace.

CXCI

Your life has great significance.

Discover the meaning of life and the reasons you are on this planet – that is your main task.

Many ignorantly believe amassing material wealth to be the reason, but once they have done so, they lose interest and experience as much frustration and unhappiness as those who have not achieved anything at all.

If you look at the spiritual issue of life, the need for self-enlightenment with the Divine Thought, your whole journey will unfold safely and productively.

No one can feel complete without being in constant connection with God, the Source of All Good.

Think this over and follow the path of life everlasting.

CXCII

There is a widespread, erroneous notion that honest, hard-working people are fools.

This comes about as a consequence of material prosperity due to injustice, theft, disgrace and bribery, which today have reached devastating proportions within society.

However, those who think and act this way are wrong. Material prosperity without dignity corrupts habits, disrupts the individual and degrades the soul.

Only honor prevails; the good outlasts everything.

Stay wise and live with dignity.

CXCIII

Deception, violence and crime seem to be victorious everywhere. These are days of absurdity and well-calculated evil.

Of course there is an avalanche of madness looming.

However, never before has earth witnessed so much love and kindness!

Scandals and disasters sell better than selflessness and common sense. Nevertheless, there are countless people who believe in others and work on their behalf, fostering the Age of Happiness.

Join these unsung heroes of the Good, helping them to be free and joyful.

Joanna de Ângelis/Divaldo Franco

CXCIV

Teach the virtues of healthy living, encouraging others to take up the challenge.

The praise for self-consuming pleasures and excesses are divulged enthusiastically.

However, the decadence of the aces and champions of misguided sex and the delusion of those who live for intoxicating experiences are seldom commented on with the same ardor…

Those who used to make the headlines in newspapers and magazines, or who used to enjoy success on the radio or television yesterday, have all faded into oblivion. They have been replaced by new pawns in the market of madness.

Live a morally wholesome life and show others how good it is.

CXCV

People aspiring to a better future for Humanity must contribute to educate and improve the lives of children.

Whatever is invested in children will be returned with interest.

The investment of love will return as saving grace, whereas abandonment will return as crime and disgrace.

If you lack specific resources to help children, at least offer them sound advice and examples that will encourage them to become good citizens when they grow up.

Build today for a better tomorrow.

Joanna de Ângelis/Divaldo Franco

CXCVI

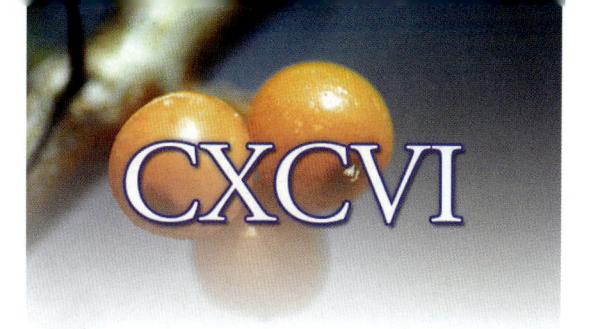

When you are about to give up on an uplifting endeavor, pray and then continue until it is finished.

When you are about to make a mistake, pray and then desist peaceably.

If you feel your strength faltering as you work for the Good, pray, take heart and finish what you've started.

When you are lured into a vexing situation, pray and retake your self-control.

When you feel abandoned by someone you love or trust, pray, be patient and stay at your post.

When you lose hope and have no motivation left, pray and you will be granted the endurance to succeed.

Never stop praying.

CXCVII

Set some time aside to recharge your mind.

Just as the body gets worn out, the mind also gets tired and misaligned.

A change in activities, leisure, sports, games and meditation – all these are valuable resources for mental readjustment.

Allocate some time for inner renewal, taking stock of what you are doing and looking for ways to make it more enjoyable, allowing for more balance and less fatigue.

The mind is a mirror that reflects the state of the Spirit. It deserves love and care to function at its peak.

CXCVIII

In whatever activity you are involved, look at yourself as being God's servant.

However humble your profession, it is extremely valuable within your social context.

Perform your duties joyfully and be aware of their worth and significance for the community.

Massive islands arise from the sea, built by insignificant polyps.

Tiny grains of sand gather to form vast deserts.

Voluminous oceans are but a collection of small drops of water.

Your contribution to the world is of great importance. Therefore, work cheerfully and do it well.

CXCIX

Don't let pessimism make you give up on the struggle.

What others obtain through work, so will you if you have patience and persevere.

Don't try to begin where others are finishing.

Success comes after many failed attempts.

Every failure teaches you how something should not be done.

Stay the course with an upbeat attitude and slowly inch your way toward success. Each day that you remain engaged means another twenty-four hours in your favor.

Joanna de Ângelis/Divaldo Franco

Thank God for your existence.
Praise God by living a wholesome life.
Exalt God's love by fulfilling your duties uprightly.
Honor God by being a devoted and faithful servant.
Introduce God to humanity by being a model friend, brother or sister in all situations.
Glorify God by working for the good of all – your brothers and sisters in humanity.
Respect God by obeying the Sovereign Laws governing life.
Acknowledge God in everything and everyone by leading a happy life as God's beloved child.